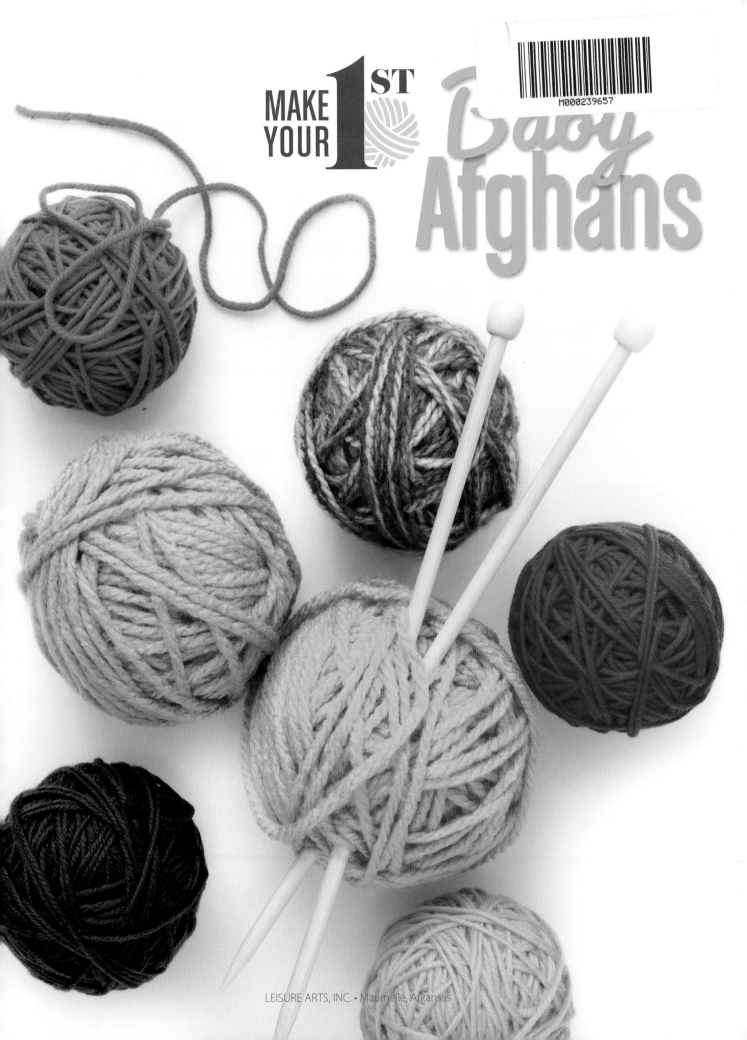

MAKE YOUR 1ST Baby Afghans

LEISURE ARTS, INC. • Maumelle, Arkansas

M000239657

Introduction

One of the main reasons so many people learn to knit is to make items for babies. When I taught knitting at my local yarn shop many new knitters would tell me they wanted to make a baby afghan for a loved one. I can remember having a conversation with one customer about her desire to make a baby afghan that would get the most ooh's and ahh's at the baby shower. It made me chuckle because I think secretly, that is the goal of most knitters.

We all have been there, sitting at a baby shower, the mom-to-be opening the gifts, then she picks up the big gift bag with a pink and purple curly ribbon on top. The mom smiles and says, "I know what this is!", then she opens the bag and pulls out the most beautiful knitted baby afghan. Everybody in the room ooh's and ahh's, and looks at the knitter and asks, "did you make that?" With a proud smile, the knitter nods her head. I'm sure the knitter is sitting there thinking, **mission accomplished**!

I know I can totally relate to both knitters; I want to make items that people love and I love making pieces for babies! That is what makes this book so perfect; it is a wonderful combination of knit baby afghan designs that are easy, fun, and relatively quick. These are sure to be a perfect gift for any baby in your life.

MEET MARLY BIRD

I honestly believe anybody can knit, it just takes a little patience and guidance to get there. I've been knitting for nearly 20 years and from the minute I learned how to do this amazing craft, I wanted to share it with others. I started a knitting and crochet group at my church, a Mommy stitching group that met at McDonald's every week, a blog and a podcast to share my passion with others. I love the fellowship with other fiber minded people and love to teach men, women and children how to work with needles and string, and watch the "a-ha!" moment in their eyes when they get it.

I want to present a series of books that hold your hand through the process of knitting various items. Things that you have been interested in making, have always wanted to make, or don't know you MUST make RIGHT NOW!

Marly Bird™

Books that will walk you through step-by-step on how to make anything from baby afghans to sweaters.

Books that offer more than just instructions but also offer tips, tricks, suggestions for how to make it your own.

Books that you will pass down to your kids to show them how you learned to knit.

"This book is a wonderful combination of knit baby afghan designs that are easy, fun, and relatively quick."

Contents

What is so great about this book? It's full of basic skill level baby afghans.

Need help?
Turn to Getting Started page 4, it will help you jump right in and tackle your first one. Of course, I've given you my favorite hints and tips! Now, have fun creating your first afghan!

Are you looking for information about needles or trying to understand the symbols?
Check out the General Instructions beginning on page 40. But, if you need a stitch refresher, you will find that in the Knitting Basics on pages 44-47.

Getting Started

This book is a great way to learn new stitches and use them to make a treasured baby afghan. Take a moment to learn how to do basic stitches, then put your knowledge to work to make a simple piece like the Garter Stitch baby afghan or the Simple Stockinette & Garter Stitch baby afghan. Once you feel comfortable, you can begin to learn more intermediate stitches and then make the Knit & Purl Weave baby afghan or the Bold Chevron baby afghan. By the time you have made the baby afghans in this book, you will be ready to make any knitting pattern or project.

Choosing yarn for your afghan is an exciting part of the knitting process. The possibilities are endless! Here are some of the top things you should consider when picking out the yarn you want to use.

WEIGHT

When following a pattern you often want to have a finished item that is similar to the sample. However, we know that there are times when you want to use a different yarn. Yes, you can do that. But, when you choose the new yarn, it is important that you pay attention to the weight of the yarn used in the sample versus the weight of your new yarn choice.

The Craft Yarn Council (CYC) has made it easy for us knitters to know the weights of yarn by assigning labels to them. We now have a standard to go by. On each of the patterns in this book, in the shopping list, you will find a symbol next to the yarn. That symbol indicates the CYC standard weight of the yarn used in the pattern. As long as you choose a yarn that has that same symbol or same weight, you should be good to go.

SUPER FINE
1
Sock, Fingering Baby

FINE
2
Sport, Baby

LIGHT
3
DK, Light Worsted

FIBER

Just as the weight of the yarn is important, so too is the fiber content. Not all fibers are the same. Each type of fiber has unique characteristics that must be taken into account when considering substitution (which is pretty much a pattern-by-pattern process).

Here are some examples:

Machine Washability

Mercerized merino, cotton and most acrylics are machine washable, but silk or pure wool are not.

A word of caution—if you change the weight of yarn for a project not only will the size of the afghan change (assuming you adjust the gauge to get what works best for the yarn you are using) but your yarn amounts will change. So be sure you have enough of the yarn you want to use.

Elasticity

This is the fiber's ability to stretch and contract, which affects an item's ability to regain its original shape. Animal fibers and some synthetics are stretchy, while plant fibers are not.

In general, the closer you stick to the recommended fiber type, the more predictable the results will be.

MEDIUM
4
Worsted, Afghan, Aran

BULKY
5
Chunky, Craft, Rug

SUPER BULKY
6
Super Bulky, Roving

JUMBO
7
Jumbo, Roving

COLOR

Color can be very intimidating and sometimes challenging for a crafter. It is a difficult thing for me as well. Here is a little tip I have to help you put colors together. When I am working on a new pattern that has multiple colors, I always take a look at the different fabrics that are available. I look for color combinations that I like or that are on-trend. When I find one, I then find a yarn with the same or similar colors and go from there. Not hard at all, right?

The good news for you is that all the designs in this book either use only one color, a variegated yarn that does all the color changes for you, or many colors that complement one another like the Garter Squares afghan. If a particular color doesn't speak to you and you wish to change it, PLEASE, DO! You officially have my permission.

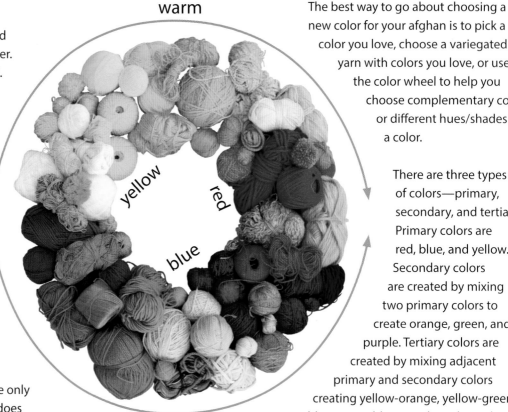

warm

yellow   red

blue

cool

The best way to go about choosing a new color for your afghan is to pick a color you love, choose a variegated yarn with colors you love, or use the color wheel to help you choose complementary colors or different hues/shades of a color.

There are three types of colors—primary, secondary, and tertiary. Primary colors are red, blue, and yellow. Secondary colors are created by mixing two primary colors to create orange, green, and purple. Tertiary colors are created by mixing adjacent primary and secondary colors creating yellow-orange, yellow-green, blue-green, blue-purple, red-purple, and red-orange.

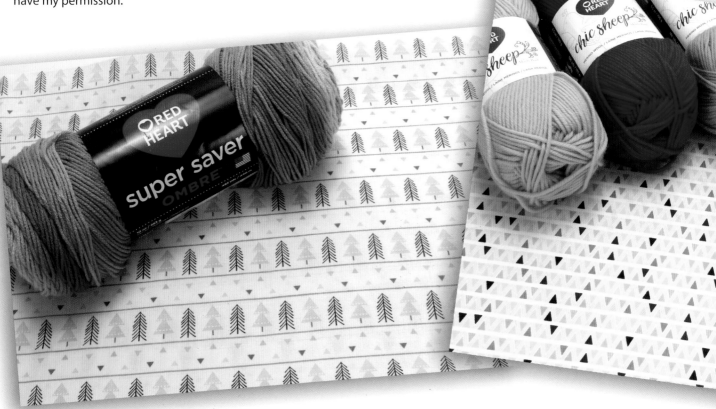

"I look for color combinations that I like or that are on-trend. When I find one, I then find a yarn with the same or similar colors and go from there."

Now that we have explored colors, you can use several colors that all have the same temperature. Warm colors are yellow, orange, and red while cool colors are green, blue, and purple.

You can select 3 colors that are next to each other on the color wheel (such as red, red-purple, and purple). You can also create a palette with one family of hues: pastels, for example, or neutrals.

Another choice is to use a tonal mood and choose several shades of a single color like burgundy, red, and pink, for instance. Then add some black, white, or cream for more depth.

GAUGE

You can knit for years without worrying about gauge, but as you expand your skills and really fine-tune your technique, you will want to follow patterns and recreate those items in both style and size. That is where the term gauge becomes very important.

Every knitted fabric is made up of stitches and rows. Gauge is the number of stitches and rows it takes to make one square inch or one full repeat of the knitted fabric. In any pattern, you will find the gauge the designer used to make that item. And, as long as you get the same number of stitches and the same number of rows to equal the measurement as written in the pattern, then you are sure to get the same size as the designer intended.

Gauge isn't always important, such as when you're making a scarf, an afghan, a bag, or anything else for which a precise size isn't essential. But when size does matter, the right or wrong gauge can make or break the finished piece.

Things that affect gauge include the yarn, the needle size and brand, and the stitch pattern you use to make your baby afghan. Yarns of different weights produce different gauges. A bulkier yarn produces a larger stitch, for example, while a finer yarn produces a smaller stitch. Needles and stitch size—the same yarn knit on different size needles will have different gauges; the same can be said of different brands of needles. Because you make a stitch by wrapping yarn around the needle, the size (circumference) of the needle determines the size of the stitch.

> " . . . when size does matter, the right or wrong gauge can make or break the finished piece."

As for the brand, different brands of needles are styled to have different points, are made of different materials, and are either shorter or longer and as a result, a knitter will knit differently with different needles. Therefore, it is important that when your gauge swatch is complete and you get a yarn and needle combination that works for you, be sure to stick with that exact needle throughout the project.

Gauge Swatches

Just as it is important to use the same needle you plan on using for your project, It is important that you use the same yarn for your gauge swatch as for your project, not the same brand in a different color. Different dyes can affect how a specific yarn knits up, and believe it or not, a yarn in one color can give you a different gauge from the same yarn in a different color.

To make your swatch, follow these steps:

1. Cast on the stitch multiple for the stitch pattern you are going to use. Guesstimate about how many multiples you need to yield a fabric that is at least 5" (12.75 cm) wide.
2. Work in the stitch pattern for the number of rows of the row pattern repeat, then enough more rows to yield 5" (12.75 cm) tall.
3. Finish off, cut the strand of yarn, leaving an 8" (20.5 cm) tail.
4. Block the swatch in the same manner you plan to use for your finished project.

Measure Gauge Swatch

To measure your swatch, smooth it out on a flat surface. Pin the edges down if they're curling in—be careful not to stretch your swatch—and follow these steps:

1. Lay a ruler along a row of stitches and mark the beginning and end of 4" (10 cm) with straight pins.
2. Note the number of stitches or stitch pattern repeats in 4" (10 cm), fractions and all.
3. Lay your ruler along a vertical line of stitches, aligning the bottom of the ruler with the bottom of a stitch, and put a straight pin in to show where the first stitch begins. Place another straight pin 4" (10 cm) up.
4. Count the rows between the pins, fractions and all, and note the number of rows.

You now know the number of stitches or stitch pattern repeats, as well as the row or row pattern repeats you get with that yarn and that needle over 4" (10 cm). Check to see if those measurements are the same as what the pattern indicates you need. If it is spot on, lucky you!

If it is off, here is what you do. If the stitches are too many, then your stitches are too small and you need to go up a needle size. If the stitches are too few, then your stitches are too big and you need to go down a needle size. Easy as that. But, work another swatch to be sure using the different size needles will work.

Blocking

For any finished item that you plan on washing at some point, you want to actually wash the swatch. Treat the swatch as you would the finished item. Use soap, put it in the washer (if it is machine washable) and let it dry. Doing so will help you see how the fabric will behave after washing. Does it hold together? Does it pill? Does it stretch? All of these things are important to know before you spend your time using that yarn to make a full-size item.

Those are the benefits of washing your swatch, but what about the blocking part? First, did you know that the given gauge in a pattern is the blocked gauge (unless noted differently)? That means, it is entirely possible to have a pre-blocked gauge of 3 stitch pattern repeats = 4" (10 cm) but after blocking the measurement can increase to 2 stitch pattern repeats = 4" (10 cm). Over the course of a full project, that is a HUGE difference. Therefore, it is imperative that you know what the blocked gauge is of your swatch.

Now, for the most part, wet blocking acrylic yarn doesn't really do anything to change it, but when you are using a wool, like Chic Sheep by Marly Bird™, blocking is very important. Specifically, I suggest wet blocking.

Just as I mentioned above, you want to wash your swatch. For wool, I suggest hand-washing the finished swatch in your sink and use a wool wash. When you do this you are giving that yarn a spa treatment. The yarn has been handled, tugged, pulled, knit and really just needs a chance to relax and let the fibers settle into place. Not only will the yarn really show its true beauty when cleaned but it will block even more beautifully.

After the swatch has had a good wash, follow these steps to block it out.

1. Get as much water out of your swatch as you can without stretching or wringing it out.
   Note: When you lift the piece out of the sink, lift it out in both hands, making sure not to let any part of it stretch down.

BLOCKING TIP
I like to use the cardboard cutting boards from the fabric section of the big box store. The grid lines on the board make it easy to measure out and block my swatch or my finished piece.

Note: Before you use it, be sure to use a damp paper towel and wipe it down to get rid of any extra ink!

2. Without stretching the piece, spread it out on the towel and fold the ends of the towel over it; then gently and loosely roll up the towel to absorb more water.
3. Gently lay your piece out on the blocking board.
4. Spread your piece out using the measurements of the piece as a guide.
5. Using straight pins, pin and smooth all pieces.
6. Allow the piece to air dry. Keep the piece out of the sun as that may cause discoloration. If you're in a hurry, you can get your piece to dry in a matter of hours by placing a fan in front of it.

The last thing to do after the swatch has been blocked is to unpin it from the blocking board, let it rest for a couple minutes then measure it for the gauge.

Here are some basic knit supplies—yarn, knitting needles, ruler, stitch markers, row counters, and yarn needles.

Yarn

Knitting needles

Stitch markers

Row counters

Ruler

Yarn needles

11

Hints & Tips

I'm a brand spanking new knitter, where do I start?

First, welcome to the best club ever! Being a knitter is AWESOME! Now, the first afghan I would start with is the Garter Stitch, and I will say make sure you pick a yarn that excites you. I made this design with a variegated yarn that is super soft and has very on-trend colors that bring joy to me.

Why is the yarn choice important?

You want to make sure you do not get bored as you're working on a project that is all garter stitch. By choosing a yarn with fun colors or long color changes, you will be excited to work with the yarn. Couple that with the joy of seeing how the colors all work together as it is knit makes for a very enjoyable experience even though you are only doing garter stitch.

Plus, this afghan is great because it is a nice and small afghan, the perfect size to tuck in a car seat and not drag on the ground.

When I add a new ball of yarn to an ombre yarn, do I start in the same color place?

When working with any yarn that has a color sequence you have to make that choice. You can certainly start at any location and let it be a design feature. Or you can start at the exact same point of color sequence on the new ball of yarn as where the old ball left off. It all depends on the look you are going for on your afghan.

Are chevron stitches giving you trouble?

When I do chevrons, I think of them as peaks and valleys. When you get to a peak of a chevron, you have to do an increase, when you are in the valley you have to do a decrease (eliminate a stitch by working two stitches together). As long as I maintain the increase at the peaks and decreases in the valleys, I am sure to get perfect chevrons.

I love this afghan but I want it to be bigger/smaller.

That is an easy one! Should you like the look of a particular afghan, like the Cartridge Stitch, but you want it to be bigger, all you have to do is increase the number of stitch multiples across and the number of rows you work.

Sticking with this afghan as the example, the pattern has you cast on 126 stitches and the stitch multiple is any number of stitches. That means if we want to double the length of the afghan, we would have to cast on 252 stitches. Then, to double the width we simply work double the number of rows in pattern.

For any of the other patterns, specifically those with stitch patterns like the Knit & Purl Weave, you must pay attention to the stitch multiple when increasing the

"*Pay attention to the stitches you are making and the pattern they create. Look at the actual fabric you are creating and understand what the stitches you are using are creating.*"

cast on number, and the row multiple when making it longer. Also, if a pattern has a border, like the Bold Chevron, you do not want to increase the total number of border stitches only the actual stitches in the body. Which means you have to calculate the stitch multiple for only the chevron pattern stitches and increase that number, leaving the border alone.

Love the stitch pattern but not the variegated yarn?

Not a problem, get a completely different look by choosing a solid color yarn to make the afghan. Or maybe choose to make an afghan in stripes instead of a solid. I think the Simple Stockinette & Garter Stitch afghan would look great in a solid color.

Save your stitches! What is a lifeline and how do I use it?

For all of you who don't know what to do when you make a mistake and have to rip out several rows, let me introduce you to lifelines!

Lifelines are truly a lifesaver when ripping out stitches, especially if you've caught a mistake that is more than a few rows down in a lace pattern. Lifelines are added to your knitting as you complete a row in the pattern that you KNOW is absolutely correct. It will give you a point to which you can rip back without the stitches falling. They won't fall because you will add a string or yarn to the row to act as a safety net or a lifeline.

Follow these instructions for adding a lifeline.

1. Use a slick, smooth strand of yarn or embroidery floss that will move nicely through your stitches.
2. Use a color that will not rub or bleed onto your fabric.
3. Thread the strand of yarn or embroidery floss (this is the lifeline) through a tapestry needle.

4. Use the needle to thread the lifeline through the stitches on your needle. Do NOT put the lifeline through the stitch markers if you have them.
5. Use caution to not split a stitch and make sure you get any and all yarn overs.

Some knitters will use lifelines every 5 or 10 rows just to be sure nothing goes wrong. There is no magic number for how many rows you have to do before adding a lifeline, it is there for you as an aid so use it as often as you wish. It helps prevent a catastrophe should something go wrong.

So, if you do find a mistake, you can rip back to the lifeline, then carefully slip the stitches back onto the needle and begin knitting again.

Don't get lost, Look At Your Work!

I know this sounds really obvious but many knitters get into a rhythm of knitting and forget to look at their work. Pay attention to the stitches you are making and the pattern they create. Instead of following a pattern blindly, look at the actual fabric and understand what the stitches you are using are creating. Doing so will help you recognize any irregularities or mistakes early. If something looks wrong with the pattern, maybe a chevron is offset or you don't have as many stitches at the end of the row as you should, you can fix the problem before it gets more compounded.

"If something looks wrong with the pattern, fix the problem before it gets more compounded."

Biggest piece of advice for beginners, Count Your Stitches!

That is right, after each row be sure to count your stitches. One stitch more or one stitch less than you cast on often means a mistake in the row you just worked. If you catch the off count early it is easy enough, albeit a little slow, to fix by tinking back that one row and redoing the row. You will not have to count forever but until you are comfortable with the needles, the yarn and the pattern, it is good practice to count.

I like to use stitch markers and either place them on the needles every 20 stitches or between every stitch repeat. That makes it easier to count overall but more importantly, with stitch markers I know sooner rather than later that I have a mistake if the count is off between stitch markers. Therefore, I only have to tink to the previous stitch marker instead of the entire row.

What is tinking?

To tink is to unknit your work stitch by stitch. If you find a mistake, you can tink back one stitch at a time to the mistake. This method is often preferred to just taking the needles out of the knitting and ripping back but it is a little more time consuming.

Follow these steps for tinking stitches.

1. Insert the left-hand needle from front to back into the stitch below the one on the right-hand needle.
2. Let the stitch on the right-hand needle fall off and gently pull the yarn so the stitch unravels from the stitch below (the one the left-hand needle is inserted into).
3. Now slide the stitch that the left-hand needle is in onto the left-hand needle more securely because it is now an unworked stitch.
4. Repeat steps 1-3 until you are to the point of the mistake.

Do I have to use circular needles?

The short answer is no; however, with the number of stitches that will be on the needles for some of the baby afghans, it is easier to manage them if you use long circular needles. Plus, when the stitches are not squished up on the needle, your knitting will be more uniform. I highly encourage you to use long circular needles as straight needles when making these baby afghans.

I hate weaving in ends... what can I do?

Well, know that you are not alone with that opinion. Not many knitters I know enjoy weaving in ends. BUT, it is a necessary evil. I am not a fan of just knitting over ends so please do not do that. Take the time to properly weave in your ends.

Oh No, there is a knot in my yarn!

Ya, it happens. You will be knitting along when all of a sudden there is a knot in the yarn from the manufacturer. Don't panic, it is just a simple little knot. The first thing I want to tell you is this, are you listening? No, really, are you listening? Okay, here it is...DO NOT KNIT OVER THE KNOT! That's right, you want to go ahead and back up to the edge of the work (I like to change colors or add new yarn at the edge whenever possible), leave yourself at least 4-6" (10-15 cm) of length, cut that yarn with the knot, then again leaving a 4-6" (10-15 cm) tail of the yarn, rejoin the yarn as you would if you were changing colors and carry on.

This makes for more ends to weave in, yes. But it also means you will have a better finished piece that

doesn't have knots in the middle of the fabric. Plus, you have no idea if those knots are secure and the last thing you want is to have the knot come undone from the baby afghan you gave as a gift, right?

I made changes, but I can't remember what I did!

This happens to me all the time; I get excited about a project or pattern and just want to work on it. Like many of you, I lie to myself by saying that I will remember what I did, then days go by, I pick up my pattern and I have no idea what I am doing.

Learn from my mistakes. The best piece of advice I can offer is to take notes as you are working on a project. If a pen and paper is your jam, great! Be sure to have a notebook next to you as you work on your afghan and jot down notes (the yarn are you using, the needle size and brand, your gauge, the title of the book and the page number of the pattern you are using, etc.).

If you are more tech savvy, then pop open an app that you can keep notes in and use that. I know that every phone, pad, tablet or whatnot has their own so I am not going to recommend any here.

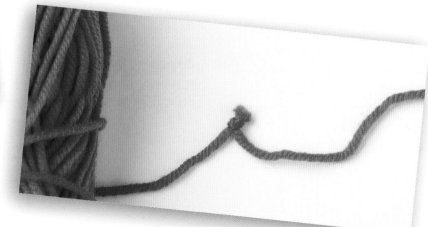

The bottom line is this, taking notes is very important when you are working on any pattern. It is a place that you can keep track of the details of your pattern or even keep a tally of the number of repeats or rows you have completed. But notes are especially important if you're making changes to a pattern.

What is Intarsia?

I made each design in this book as an introduction to a particular stitch or technique. One of those is basic intarsia. The Waves of Cables baby afghan has color changes in the body, but you will notice that the border is the same color throughout. This is done by working a technique called intarsia.

Basically, you will work each color section in a row with its own ball of yarn. When changing colors, you bring the new color up from underneath the old one. This twists the strands together,

preventing holes from forming on the front of the work. Then you leave the old strand of yarn hanging and continue on in pattern. Each time you change colors in an intarsia design, you do it the same way, regardless of whether you are working from the right or wrong side of the piece. Also, as you change from one ball to the next, you will overlap the two colors on the wrong side of the fabric to lock it in place.

It isn't as hard as it might sound, I encourage you to give it a try! The Waves of Cables baby afghan is an excellent way to start!

How to count cable rows

I thinking counting rows between cables is a difficult thing to do, so I use the aid of a split-ring stitch marker. I will place

a stitch marker in a stitch at the edge of my work ON the row that is an actual cable row. Leave the stitch marker in place and continue in pattern. Now, as I am working, I can look at the placement of that stitch marker and count the number of rows from that point to know if I am on a cable row or not.

For example, the Waves of Cables pattern has a cable row every 4 rows. If I place a stitch marker at the start of Row 5, and continue to work along, when I get to Row 9 and I am unsure that I have done the correct number of rows, I can count the number of rows up from that stitch marker to know if I am beginning the fourth row since the last cable row.

Easy peasy!

Garter Stitch

GAUGE INFORMATION

In Garter Stitch (knit every row),
    16 sts and 36 rows = 4" (10 cm)

Afghan

Cast on 115 sts.

Work in Garter Stitch (knit every row)
until piece measures approximately 25"
(63.5 cm) from cast on edge.

Bind off all sts in **knit**.

Finished Size:
28¾" x 25"
(73 cm x 63.5 cm)

BASIC

Finished Size:
28½" x 36"
(72.5 cm x 91.5 cm)

GAUGE INFORMATION
In pattern,
    14 sts and 27 rows = 4" (10 cm)

Afghan
Cast on 126 sts.

Row 1 (Right side)**:** Knit across.

Row 2: Purl across.

Rows 3 and 4: Knit across.

Row 5: Purl across.

Rows 6 and 7: Knit across.

Repeat Rows 2-7 for pattern until piece measures approximately 28½" (72.5 cm) from cast on edge, ending by working Row 6.

Bind off all sts in **purl**.

Simple Stockinette & Garter Stitch

BASIC

Finished Size:
47½" x 39¼"
(120.5 cm x 99.5 cm)

GAUGE INFORMATION

In Stockinette Stitch
   (knit one row, purl one row),
   13 sts and 18 rows = 4" (10 cm)
In pattern, one row repeat
   (20 rows) = 3¾" (9.5 cm)

Afghan

With Color A, cast on 154 sts.

Rows 1-10: Knit across; at end of Row 10, cut Color A.

Row 11 (Right side)**:** With Color B, K 10, place marker *(see Markers, page 42)*, knit across to last 10 sts, place marker, K 10.

Row 12: Knit across to next marker, slip marker, purl across to next marker, slip marker, knit across.

Row 13: (Knit across to next marker, slip marker) twice, knit across.

Rows 14-20: Repeat Rows 12 and 13, 3 times; then repeat Row 12 once **more**; at end of Row 20, cut Color B.

Rows 21-30: With Color A, (knit across to next marker, slip marker) twice, knit across; at end of Row 30, cut Color A.

Repeat Rows 11-30 for pattern until piece measures approximately 39" (99 cm) from cast on edge, ending by working Row 30; do **not** cut Color A.

Bind off all sts in **knit** removing markers.

Knit & Purl Weave

Finished Size:
31¼" x 39"
(79.5 cm x 99 cm)

GAUGE INFORMATION

In pattern, 10 sts = 4" (10 cm);
  one repeat (12 rows) = 3¼"
  (8.25 cm)

Afghan

Cast on 78 sts.

Row 1 (Right side)**:** K2, P2, K2, (P6, K2, P2, K2) across.

Row 2: P2, K2, P2, (K6, P2, K2, P2) across.

Row 3: K2, P2, (K 10, P2) across to last 2 sts, K2.

Row 4: P2, K2, (P 10, K2) across to last 2 sts, P2.

Row 5: K8, P2, (K 10, P2) across to last 8 sts, K8.

Row 6: P8, K2, (P 10, K2) across to last 8 sts, P8.

Row 7: P6, (K2, P2, K2, P6) across.

Row 8: K6, (P2, K2, P2, K6) across.

Row 9: K8, P2, (K 10, P2) across to last 8 sts, K8.

Row 10: P8, K2, (P 10, K2) across to last 8 sts, P8.

Row 11: K2, P2, (K 10, P2) across to last 2 sts, K2.

Row 12: P2, K2, (P 10, K2) across to last 2 sts, P2.

Repeat Rows 1-12 for pattern until piece measures approximately 39" (99 cm) from cast on edge, ending by working Row 12.

Bind off all sts in **knit**.

Shopping List
Yarn (Super Bulky Weight)

[3.5 ounces, 89 yards
(100 grams, 81 meters)
per skein]:
☐ 6 skeins

Knitting Needle
36" (91.5 cm) Circular,
☐ Size 13 (9 mm)
  or size needed for gauge

Simple Reversible

Finished Size:
43" (108 cm) square

GAUGE INFORMATION
In pattern,
3 repeats (18 sts) and
5 repeats (30 rows) = 5¼" (13.5 cm)

Afghan
Border
Cast on 154 sts.

Rows 1-8: Knit across.

Row 9: K5, place marker *(see Markers, page 42)*, knit across to last 5 sts, place marker, K5.

Body
Row 1 (Right side)**:** Knit across to next marker, slip marker, (K4, P2) across to next marker, slip marker, knit across.

Row 2: Knit across to next marker, slip marker, (K2, P4) across to next marker, slip marker, knit across.

Row 3: Knit across to next marker, slip marker, (K4, P2) across to next marker, slip marker, knit across.

Row 4: Knit across to next marker, slip marker, (P2, K4) across to next marker, slip marker, knit across.

Row 5: Knit across to next marker, slip marker, (P4, K2) across to next marker, slip marker, knit across.

Row 6: Knit across to next marker, slip marker, (P2, K4) across to next marker, slip marker, knit across.

Repeat Rows 1-6 for pattern until piece measures approximately 41½" (105.5 cm) from cast on edge, ending by working Row 6.

Border
Row 1: Knit across removing markers.

Rows 2-9: Knit across.

Bind off all sts in **knit**.

Shopping List
Yarn (Medium Weight)

MEDIUM
4

[5 ounces, 223 yards (141 grams, 204 meters) per skein]:
☐ 6 skeins

Knitting Needle
36" (91.5 cm) Circular,
☐ Size 10 (6 mm)
   or size needed for gauge

Additional Supplies
☐ Stitch markers - 2

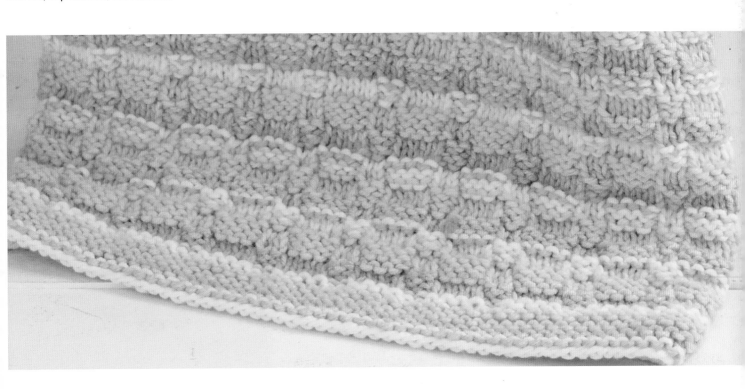

Garter Squares

BASIC

Afghan
Strips #1 & #7

With Color E, cast on 22 sts.

Rows 1-42: Knit across.

Cut Color E.

Rows 43-84: With Color D, knit across.

Cut Color D.

Rows 85-126: With Color B, knit across.

Cut Color B.

Rows 127-168: With Color C, knit across.

Cut Color C.

Rows 169-210: With Color B, knit across.

Cut Color B.

Rows 211-252: With Color D, knit across.

Cut Color D.

Rows 253-294: With Color E, knit across.

Bind off all sts in **knit**.

Strips #2 & #6

With Color D, cast on 22 sts.

Rows 1-42: Knit across.

Cut Color D.

Rows 43-84: With Color B, knit across.

Cut Color B.

Rows 85-126: With Color C, knit across.

Cut Color C.

Rows 127-168: With Color A, knit across.

Cut Color A.

Rows 169-210: With Color C, knit across.

Cut Color C.

Rows 211-252: With Color B, knit across.

Cut Color B.

Rows 253-294: With Color D, knit across.

Bind off all sts in **knit**.

Strips #3 & #5
With Color B, cast on 22 sts.

Rows 1-42: Knit across.

Cut Color B.

Rows 43-84: With Color C, knit across.

Cut Color C.

Rows 85-126: WIth Color A, knit across.

Cut Color A.

Rows 127-168: With Color E, knit across.

Cut Color E.

Rows 169-210: With Color A, knit across.

Cut Color A.

Rows 211-252: With Color C, knit across.

Cut Color C.

Rows 253-294: With Color B, knit across.

Bind off all sts in **knit**.

Strip #4
With Color C, cast on 22 sts.

Rows 1-42: Knit across.

Cut Color C.

Rows 43-84: With Color A, knit across.

Cut Color A.

Rows 85-126: With Color E, knit across.

Cut Color E.

Rows 127-168: With Color D, knit across.

Cut Color D.

Rows 169-210: With Color E, knit across.

Cut Color E.

Rows 211-252: With Color A, knit across.

Cut Color A.

Rows 253-294: With Color C, knit across.

Bind off all sts in **knit**.

Assembly
Having all cast on edges at the same end and Strips in numerical order, weave Strips together with matching colors *(Fig. 7, page 43)*.

Borders
BOTTOM
With **right** side facing and Color A, pick up 22 sts evenly spaced across cast on edges of each Strip *(Fig. 6b, page 43)*: 154 sts.

Rows 1-7: Knit across.

Bind off all sts in **knit**.

TOP
Work same as Bottom on bound off edges of each Strip.

FIRST SIDE
With **right** side facing and Color A, pick up 4 sts evenly spaced across ends of rows of Border *(Fig. 6a, page 43)*, pick up 21 sts evenly spaced across each color section of Strip, pick up 4 sts evenly spaced across ends of rows of Border: 155 sts.

Rows 1-7: Knit across.

Bind off all sts in **knit**.

SECOND SIDE
Work same as First Side on opposite edge of Afghan.

Bold Chevron

BASIC

Shopping List
Yarn (Bulky Weight)

[5 ounces, 173 yards
(141 grams, 158 meters)
per skein]:
☐ Color A (Pink) - 2 skeins
☐ Color B (Teal) - 1 skein
☐ Color C (Gold) - 1 skein
☐ Color D (Blue) - 1 skein

Knitting Needle
36" (91.5 cm) Circular,
☐ Size 10 (6 mm)
  or size needed for gauge

Additional Supplies
☐ Stitch markers - 2

Finished Size:
26¼" x 32"
(66.5 cm x 81.5 cm)

GAUGE INFORMATION

In pattern, one repeat (16 sts) and
    15 rows = 4" (10 cm)

TECHNIQUES USED
• YO *(Fig. 1, page 42)*
• K3 tog *(Fig. 3, page 42)*

STRIPE SEQUENCE
Work 24 rows **each** of Color A, Color B,
Color C, Color D, **and** 22 rows Color A.

Afghan
With Color A, cast on 105 sts.

Row 1 (Right side)**:** Knit across.

Row 2: K4, place marker *(see Markers, page 42)*, knit across to last 4 sts, place marker, K4.

Row 3: Knit across to next marker, slip marker, K1, ★ YO, K6, K3 tog, K6, YO, K1; repeat from ★ across to next marker, slip marker, knit across.

Row 4: Knit across to next marker, slip marker, purl across to next marker, slip marker, knit across.

Rows 5-118: Following Stripe Sequence, repeat Rows 3 and 4, 57 times.

Row 119: With Color A, knit across removing markers.

Row 120: Knit across.

Bind off all sts in **knit** removing markers.

Finished Size:
27" x 35"
(68.5 cm x 89 cm)

GAUGE INFORMATION

In Stockinette Stitch
(knit one row, purl one row),
17 sts and 25 rows = 4" (10 cm)

TECHNIQUES USED

• YO (*Fig. 1, page 42*)
• K2 tog (*Fig. 2, page 42*)
• SSK (*Figs. 4a-c, page 42*)

Afghan

Border

Cast on 115 sts.

Rows 1-9: Knit across.

Body

Row 1: K5, place marker (*see Markers, page 42*), purl across to last 5 sts, place marker, K5.

Row 2 (Right side)**:** (Knit across to next marker, slip marker) twice, knit across.

Row 3: Knit across to next marker, slip marker, purl across to next marker, slip marker, knit across.

Row 4: Knit across to next marker, slip marker, K5, ★ K2 tog, YO, K1, YO, SSK, K5; repeat from ★ across to next marker, slip marker, knit across.

Row 5: Knit across to next marker, slip marker, purl across to next marker, slip marker, knit across.

Rows 6 and 7: Repeat Rows 4 and 5.

Row 8: (Knit across to next marker, slip marker) twice, knit across.

Row 9: Knit across to next marker, slip marker, purl across to next marker, slip marker, knit across.

Row 10: Knit across to next marker, K 10, K2 tog, YO, K1, YO, SSK, ★ K5, K2 tog, YO, K1, YO, SSK; repeat from ★ across to within 10 sts of next marker, K 10, slip marker, knit across.

Row 11: Knit across to next marker, slip marker, purl across to next marker, slip marker, knit across.

Rows 12 and 13: Repeat Rows 10 and 11.

Row 14: (Knit across to next marker, slip marker) twice, knit across.

Row 15: Knit across to next marker, slip marker, purl across to next marker, slip marker, knit across.

Rows 16-207: Repeat Rows 4-15, 16 times.

Border

Row 1: Knit across removing markers.

Rows 2-9: Knit across.

Bind off all sts in **knit**.

Ombre Lace

Finished Size:
42½" x 36½"
(108 cm x 92.5 cm)

GAUGE INFORMATION
In pattern,
  2 repeats (12 sts) = 3¼" (8.25 cm);
  one repeat (12 rows) = 2" (5 cm)

TECHNIQUES USED
• YO *(Fig. 1, page 42)*
• K2 tog *(Fig. 2, page 42)*
• SSK *(Figs. 4a-c, page 42)*

Afghan
Border
Cast on 157 sts.

Rows 1-8: Knit across.

Row 9: K6, place marker *(see Markers, page 42)*, knit across to last 6 sts, place marker, K6.

Body
Row 1 (Right side)**:** Knit across to next marker, slip marker, SSK, K2, ★ YO, K2, SSK, K2; repeat from ★ across to within 3 sts of next marker, YO, K3, slip marker, knit across.

Row 2: Knit across to next marker, slip marker, purl across to next marker, slip marker, knit across.

Rows 3-6: Repeat Rows 1 and 2 twice.

Row 7: Knit across to next marker, slip marker, K3, YO, K2, K2 tog, ★ K2, YO, K2, K2 tog; repeat from ★ across to next marker, slip marker, knit across.

Row 8: Knit across to next marker, slip marker, purl across to next marker, slip marker, knit across.

Rows 9-12: Repeat Rows 7 and 8 twice.

Rows 13-204: Repeat Rows 1-12, 16 times.

Border
Row 1: Knit across removing markers.

Rows 2-9: Knit across.

Bind off all sts in **knit**.

Shopping List
Yarn (Medium Weight)

[10 ounces, 482 yards
(283 grams, 440 meters)
per skein]:
☐ 2 skeins

Knitting Needle
40" (101.5 cm) Circular,
☐ Size 9 (5.5 mm)
  or size needed for gauge

Additional Supplies
☐ Stitch markers - 2

Waves of Cables

BASIC

Shopping List

Yarn (Jumbo Weight)

[5.29 ounces, 46 yards
(150 grams, 42 meters)
per skein]:
- ☐ Color A (Mint) - 4 skeins
- ☐ Color B (Orchid) - 2 skeins
- ☐ Color C (Green) - 2 skeins

Knitting Needle

36" (91.5 cm) Circular,
- ☐ Size 17 (12.75 mm)
  or size needed for gauge

Additional Supplies

- ☐ Stitch markers - 2
- ☐ Cable needle

Finished Size:
29½" x 34"
(75 cm x 86.5 cm)

GAUGE INFORMATION

In Cable pattern,
7 sts and 10 rows = 4" (10 cm)

STITCH GUIDE

CABLE 4 BACK (abbreviated C4B)
(uses next 4 sts)
Slip next 2 sts onto cable needle and
hold in **back** of work, K2 from left needle,
K2 from cable needle.

CABLE 4 FRONT (abbreviated C4F)
(uses next 4 sts)
Slip next 2 sts onto cable needle and
hold in **front** of work, K2 from left
needle, K2 from cable needle.

Afghan

Border

With Color A, cast on 52 sts.

Rows 1 and 2: Knit across.

Row 3: K4, place marker (**see Markers, page 42**), knit across to last 4 sts, place marker, K4.

Body

Row 1 (Right side): (Knit across to next marker, slip marker) twice, knit across.

Row 2: Knit across to next marker, slip marker, purl across to next marker, slip marker, knit across.

Rows 3 and 4: Repeat Rows 1 and 2.

Row 5: Knit across to next marker, slip marker, K2, C4B, (K4, C4B) across to within 6 sts of next marker, K6, slip marker, knit across.

Row 6: Knit across to next marker, slip marker, purl across to next marker, slip marker, knit across.

Row 7: (Knit across to next marker, slip marker) twice, knit across.

Row 8: Knit across to next marker, slip marker, purl across to next marker, slip marker, knit across.

Row 9: Knit across to next marker, slip marker, K6, C4F, (K4, C4F) across to within 2 sts of next marker, K2, slip marker, knit across.

Row 10: Knit across to next marker, slip marker, purl across to next marker, slip marker, knit across.

Row 11: (Knit across to next marker, slip marker) twice, knit across.

Row 12: Knit across to next marker, slip marker, purl across to next marker, slip marker, knit across.

Rows 13-19: Repeat Rows 5-11.

Both side borders are worked at the same time, using separate yarn for **each** side through Row 59.

Row 20: Knit across to next marker, slip marker, with Color B (**Fig. 5, page 43**), purl across to next marker, slip marker, with next Color A knit across.

Row 21: Knit across to next marker, slip marker, with Color B K2, C4B, (K4, C4B) across to within 6 sts of next marker, K6, slip marker, with next Color A knit across.

Row 22: Knit across to next marker, slip marker, with Color B purl across to next marker, slip marker, with next Color A knit across.

Row 23: Knit across to next marker, slip marker, with Color B knit across to next marker, slip marker, with next Color A knit across.

Row 24: Knit across to next marker, slip marker, with Color B purl across to next marker, slip marker, with next Color A knit across.

Row 25: Knit across to next marker, slip marker, with Color B K6, C4F, (K4, C4F) across to within 2 sts of next marker, K2, slip marker, with next Color A knit across.

Row 26: Knit across to next marker, slip marker, with Color B purl across to next marker, slip marker, with next Color A knit across.

Row 27: Knit across to next marker, slip marker, with Color B knit across to next marker, slip marker, with next Color A knit across.

Row 28: Knit across to next marker, slip marker, with Color B purl across to next marker, slip marker, with next Color A knit across.

Rows 29-39: Repeat Rows 21-28 once, then repeat Rows 21-23 once **more**; at end of Row 39, cut Color B.

Row 40: Knit across to next marker, slip marker, with Color C purl across to next marker, slip marker, with next Color A knit across.

Row 41: Knit across to next marker, slip marker, with Color C K6, C4F, (K4, C4F) across to within 2 sts of next marker, K2, slip marker, with next Color A knit across.

Row 42: Knit across to next marker, slip marker, with Color C purl across to next marker, slip marker, with next Color A knit across.

Row 43: Knit across to next marker, slip marker, with Color C knit across to next marker, slip marker, with next Color A knit across.

Row 44: Knit across to next marker, slip marker, with Color C purl across to next marker, slip marker, with next Color A knit across.

Row 45: Knit across to next marker, slip marker, with Color C, K2, C4B, (K4, C4B) across to within 6 sts of next marker, K6, slip marker, with next Color A knit across.

Row 46: Knit across to next marker, slip marker, with Color C purl across to next marker, slip marker, with next Color A knit across.

Row 47: Knit across to next marker, slip marker, with Color C knit across to next marker, slip marker, with next Color A knit across.

Row 48: Knit across to next marker, slip marker, with Color C purl across to next marker, slip marker, with next Color A knit across.

Rows 49-59: Repeat Rows 41-48 once, then repeat Rows 41-43 once **more**; at end of Row 59, cut Color C.

Row 60: Knit across to next marker, slip marker, purl across to next marker, slip marker, knit across; cut second Color A.

Rows 61-78: Repeat Rows 5-12 twice, then repeat Rows 5 and 6 once **more**.

Border
Row 1: Knit across removing markers.

Rows 2 and 3: Knit across.

Bind off all sts in **knit**.

General
Instructions

ABBREVIATIONS

C4B	Cable 4 Back
C4F	Cable 4 Front
cm	centimeters
K	knit
mm	millimeters
P	purl
SSK	slip, slip, knit
st(s)	stitch(es)
tog	together
YO	yarn over

SYMBOLS & TERMS

★ — work instructions following ★ as many **more** times as indicated in addition to the first time.

( ) or [ ] — work enclosed instructions **as many** times as specified by the number immediately following **or** contains explanatory remarks.

colon (:) — the number given after a colon at the end of a row denotes the number of stitches you should have on that row.

GAUGE

Exact gauge is **essential** for proper size. Before beginning your project, make a sample swatch in the yarn and needle specified in the individual instructions. After completing the swatch, measure it, counting your stitches and rows carefully. If your swatch is larger or smaller than specified, **make another, changing needle size to get the correct gauge.** Keep trying until you find the size needle(s) that will give you the specified gauge.

KNIT TERMINOLOGY	
UNITED STATES	**INTERNATIONAL**
gauge =	tension
bind off =	cast off
yarn over (YO) =	yarn forward (yfwd) **or** yarn around needle (yrn)

Yarn Weight Symbol & Names	LACE 0	SUPER FINE 1	FINE 2	LIGHT 3	MEDIUM 4	BULKY 5	SUPER BULKY 6	JUMBO 7
Type of Yarns in Category	Fingering, size 10 crochet thread	Sock, Fingering, Baby	Sport, Baby	DK, Light Worsted	Worsted, Afghan, Aran	Chunky, Craft, Rug	Super Bulky, Roving	Jumbo, Roving
Knit Gauge Ranges in Stockinette St to 4" (10 cm)	33-40 sts**	27-32 sts	23-26 sts	21-24 sts	16-20 sts	12-15 sts	7-11 sts	6 sts and fewer
Advised Needle Size Range	000 to 1	1 to 3	3 to 5	5 to 7	7 to 9	9 to11	11 to 17	17 and larger

* GUIDELINES ONLY: The chart above reflects the most commonly used gauges and needle sizes for specific yarn categories.

** Lace weight yarns are usually knitted on larger needles to create lacy openwork patterns. Accordingly, a gauge range is difficult to determine. Always follow the gauge stated in your pattern.

■□□□ BASIC		Projects using basic stitches. May include basic increases and decreases.
■■□□ EASY		Projects may include simple stitch patterns, color work, and/or shaping.
■■■□ INTERMEDIATE		Projects may include involved stitch patterns, color work, and/or shaping.
■■■■ COMPLEX		Projects may include complex stitch patterns, color work, and/or shaping using a variety of techniques and stitches simultaneously.

KNITTING NEEDLES																
U.S.	0	1	2	3	4	5	6	7	8	9	10	10½	11	13	15	17
U.K.	13	12	11	10	9	8	7	6	5	4	3	2	1	00	000	---
Metric - mm	2	2.25	2.75	3.25	3.5	3.75	4	4.5	5	5.5	6	6.5	8	9	10	12.75

MARKERS

As a convenience to you, we have used markers to help distinguish the beginning of a pattern. Place markers as instructed. You may use purchased markers or tie a length of contrasting color yarn around the needle. When you reach a marker on each row, slip it from the left needle to the right needle; remove it when no longer needed.

YARN OVER

(abbreviated YO)

Bring the yarn forward between the needles, then back **over** the top of the right hand needle, so that it is now in position to knit the next stitch *(Fig. 1)*.

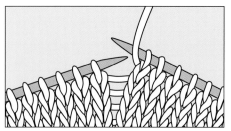

Fig. 1

DECREASES
Knit 2 Together

(abbreviated K2 tog)

Insert the right needle into the **front** of the first two stitches on the left needle as if to **knit** *(Fig. 2)*, then **knit** them together as if they were one stitch.

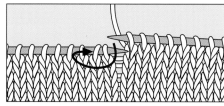

Fig. 2

Knit 3 Together

(abbreviated K3 tog)

Insert the right needle into the **front** of the first three stitches on the left needle as if to **knit** *(Fig. 3)*, then **knit** them together as if they were one stitch.

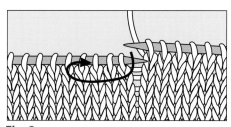

Fig. 3

Slip, Slip, Knit

(abbreviated SSK)

With yarn in **back** of work, separately slip two stitches as if to **knit** *(Fig. 4a)*. Insert the **left** needle into the **front** of both slipped stitches *(Fig. 4b)* and **knit** them together as if they were one stitch *(Fig. 4c)*.

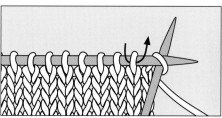

Fig. 4a

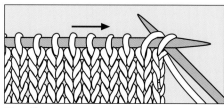

Fig. 4b

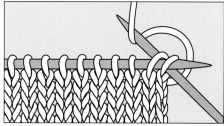

Fig. 4c

CHANGING COLORS

When changing colors, always pick up the new color yarn from **beneath** the dropped yarn and keep the color which has just been worked to the left of the new yarn *(Fig. 5)*. This will prevent holes in the finished piece.

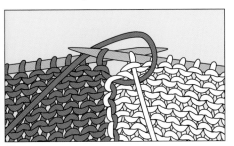

Fig. 5

PICKING UP STITCHES

When instructed to pick up stitches, insert the needle from the **front** to the **back** under two strands at the edge of the worked piece *(Figs. 6a & b)*. Put the yarn around the needle as if to **knit**, then bring the needle with the yarn back through the stitch to the right side, resulting in a stitch on the needle. Repeat this along the edge, picking up the required number of stitches. A crochet hook may be helpful to pull yarn through.

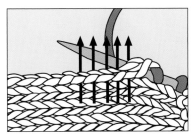

Fig. 6a

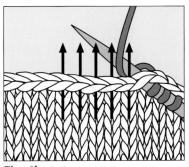

Fig. 6b

WEAVING SEAMS

With the **right** side of both pieces facing you and edges even, sew through both sides once to secure the seam. Insert the needle under the bar **between** the first and second stitches on the row and pull the yarn through *(Fig. 7)*. Insert the needle under the next bar on the second side. Repeat from side to side, being careful to match rows. If the edges are different lengths, it may be necessary to insert the needle under two bars at one edge.

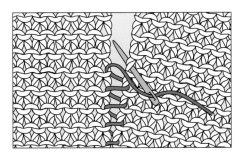

Fig. 7

Knitting Basics

SLIP KNOT

Step 1: Make a circle and place the working yarn (the yarn coming from the ball) under the circle *(Fig. 8a)*.

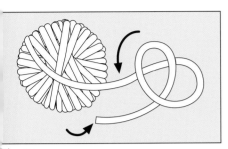

Fig. 8a

Step 2: Insert the needle under the bar just made *(Fig. 8b)* and pull on both ends of the yarn to complete the slip knot *(Fig. 8c)*. The slip knot counts as your first cast on stitch.

Fig. 8b

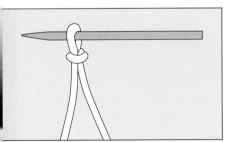

Fig. 8c

SLINGSHOT CAST ON

Step 1: Pull a length of yarn from the skein, allowing approximately 1" (2.5 cm) of yarn for each stitch to be cast on. Make a slip knot at the measured distance, pulling gently on both yarn ends to tighten stitch on needle.

Step 2: Hold the needle in your right hand with your index finger resting on the slip knot.

Step 3: Place the short end of the yarn over your left thumb, and bring the working yarn up and over your left index finger. Hold both yarn ends in your left palm with your 3 remaining fingers *(Fig. 9a)*.

Fig. 9a

Step 4: Insert the tip of the needle **under** the first strand of yarn on your left thumb *(Fig. 9b)*.

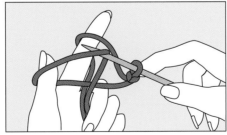

Fig. 9b

Step 5: Bring the needle **over** and around the first strand on your index finger *(Fig. 9c)*.

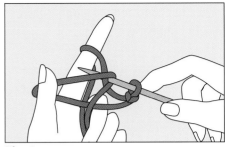

Fig. 9c

Step 6: Pull the yarn and needle down through the loop on your thumb *(Fig. 9d)*.

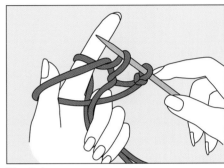

Fig. 9d

Step 7: Slip your thumb out of the loop and bring it toward you, catching the yarn end to form a new loop on your thumb *(Fig. 9e)*, and gently pulling to tighten the new stitch on the needle. Rest your index finger on the new stitch.

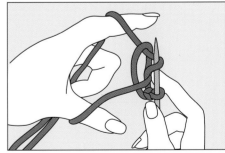

Fig. 9e

Repeat Steps 4-7 for each additional stitch.

KNIT STITCH
(abbreviated K)

Step 1: Hold the needle with the stitches in your left hand and the empty needle in your right hand.

Step 2: With the working yarn in **back** of the needles, insert the right needle into the stitch closest to the tip of the left needle as shown in *Fig. 10a*.

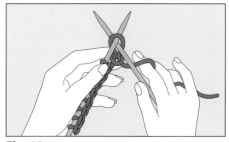

Fig. 10a

Step 3: Hold the right needle with your left thumb and index finger while you bring the yarn beneath the right needle and between the needles from **back** to **front** *(Fig. 10b)*.

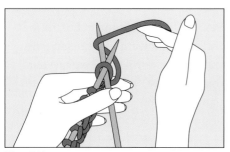

Fig. 10b

Step 4: With your right hand, bring the right needle (with the loop of yarn) toward you and through the stitch *(Figs. 10c & d)*, slip the old stitch off the left needle and gently pull to tighten the new stitch on the shaft of the right needle.

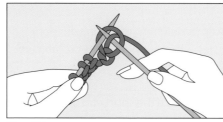

Fig. 10c

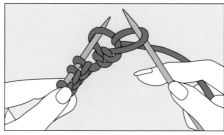

Fig. 10d

PURL STITCH
(abbreviated P)

Step 1: Hold the needle with the stitches in your left hand and the empty needle in your right hand.

Step 2: With the yarn in **front** of the needles, insert the right needle into the front of the stitch as shown in *Fig. 11a*.

Fig. 11a

Step 3: Hold the right needle with your left thumb and index finger while you bring the yarn **between** the needles from **right** to **left** and around the right needle *(Fig. 11b)*.

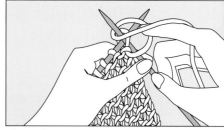

Fig. 11b

Step 4: Move the right needle (with the loop of yarn) through the stitch and away from you *(Fig. 11c)*, slip the old stitch off the left needle and gently pull to tighten the new stitch on the shaft of the right needle.

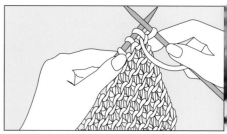

Fig. 11c

BIND OFF

Binding off is the method used to remove and secure your stitches from the knitting needles so that they don't unravel.

Work the first two stitches.

Use your left needle as a tool to lift the second stitch on the right needle up and over the first stitch (*Fig. 12a*) and completely off the right needle (*Fig. 12b*). Don't forget to remove the left needle from the stitch.

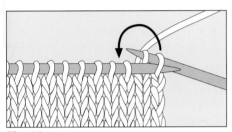

Fig. 12a

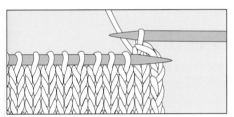

Fig. 12b

You now have one stitch on your right needle and you have bound off one stitch. Count the stitch as you bind it off, not as you work it.

Work the next stitch; you will have two stitches on your right needle. Bind off as before.

Continue until your left needle is empty and there is only one stitch left on your right needle.

Cut the yarn, leaving a long end to hide later.

Slip the stitch off the right needle, pull the end through the stitch (*Fig. 12c*) and tighten the stitch.

Fig. 12c

WEAVE IN YARN ENDS

Thread the yarn needle with the long end and weave the needle through the stitches on the **wrong** side of your piece.

Reverse the direction that you are weaving the end several times until it is securely hidden (*Fig. 13*). Clip the end off close to the work.

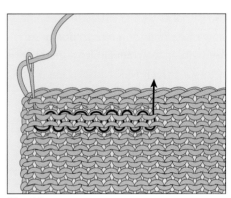

Fig. 13

Yarn Information

The Baby Afghans in this book were made using various weights of yarn. Any brand of the specified weight of yarn may be used. It is best to refer to the yardage/meters when determining how many balls or skeins to purchase. Remember, to achieve the finished size, it is the GAUGE/TENSION that is important, not the brand of yarn.

For your convenience, the specific yarns used to create our photography models are listed. Because yarn manufacturers make frequent changes in their product lines, you may sometimes find it necessary to use a substitute yarn or to search for the discontinued product at alternate suppliers (locally or online).

GARTER STITCH
Red Heart® Hopscotch™
#7958 Kickball

CARTRIDGE STITCH
Red Heart® Super Saver Ombré™
#3985 Deep Teal

SIMPLE STOCKINETTE & GARTER STITCH
Red Heart® Super Saver Chunky™
Color A (Coral) - #259 Flamingo
Color B (Green) - #520 Minty

KNIT & PURL WEAVE
Red Heart® Evermore™
#9933 Cotton Candy

SIMPLE REVERSIBLE
Red Heart® With Love Stripes™
#1973 Candy Stripe

GARTER SQUARES
Red Heart® Chic Sheep by Marly Bird™
Lt Teal - #5635 Crème de Mint
Rose - #5622 Dragon Fruit
Teal - #5693 Poolside
Purple - #5665 Royal
Green - #5620 Green Tea

BOLD CHEVRON
Red Heart® Super Saver Chunky™
Color A (Pink) - #705 Grenadine
Color B (Teal) - #656 Real Teal
Color C (Gold) - #321 Goldenrod
Color D (Blue) - #512 Turqua

BUTTERFLY KISSES
Red Heart® Baby Hugs™ Medium
#4258 Peachie

OMBRE LACE
Red Heart® Super Saver Ombré™
#3966 Jazzy

WAVES OF CABLES
Red Heart® Grande™
Color A (Mint) - #511 Wintergreen
Color B (Green) - #623 Spearmint
Color C (Orchid) - #565 Orchid

We have made every effort to ensure that these instructions are accurate and complete. We cannot, however, be responsible for human error, typographical mistakes, or variations in individual work.

Production Team: Instructional/Technical Editors - Linda A. Daley and Lois J. Long; ; Senior Graphic Artist - Lora Puls; Graphic Artist - Lori S. Malkin; Photo Stylist - Lori Wenger; and Photographer - Jason Masters.